COME, FOLLOW ME

{ A Year of Prepared Family Night Lessons
and Activities to Strengthen Your Home }

Kimiko Christensen Hammari

CFI
An imprint of Cedar Fort, Inc.
Springville, Utah

ISBN 13: 978-1-4621-2279-0

Published by CFI, an imprint of Cedar Fort, Inc., 2373 W. 700 S., Springville, UT, 84663
Distributed by Cedar Fort, Inc., www.cedarfort.com

Library of Congress Control Number: 2018959488

Cover design by Shawnda T. Craig
Cover design © 2019 Cedar Fort, Inc.
Edited by Heather Holm

Printed in the United States of America

10 9 8 7 6 5 4 3 2 1

Printed on acid-free paper

CONTENTS

How to Use This Book . . . vii

January

Heavenly Father Prepared a Way for Me
to Return to His Presence . . . 1

February

Heavenly Father Has a Plan
for His Children . . . 15

March

Jesus Christ Is Our Savior . . . 29

April

The Family Is Central to God's Plan . . . 39

May

Families Are Blessed When They
Follow the Prophet . . . 51

June

Priesthood Ordinances and Temple
Work Bless My Family . . . 61

July

We Become Members of the Church
through Baptism and Confirmation . . . 73

August

Participating in Wholesome Activities
Will Strengthen My Family . . . 85

September

Living the Gospel Blesses My Family . . . 97

October

"The Family: A Proclamation to the World"
Came from God to Help My Family . . . 113

November

Living the Teachings of Jesus Christ
Strengthens Me and My Family . . . 123

December

We Remember and Worship
Our Savior, Jesus Christ . . . 133

Answer Key . . . 145

Fun Treats for FHE

Simple, Kid-Friendly Recipes . . . 147

HOW TO USE THIS BOOK

This book provides a year's worth of family home evening lessons. The lessons are divided into monthly themes and subdivided into weekly themes. Four lessons are provided for most months. Each lesson is divided into the following sections:

Resources

Primary songs, hymns, scriptures, and pictures from the *Gospel Art Book*. (Note: The *Gospel Art Book* is available at lds.org. You can download and print pictures, or show the pictures to your children on a computer or another electronic device. You can order a copy of the *Gospel Art Book* at store.lds.org.) Pick one Primary song, one hymn, one scripture, and one picture to use during your lesson.

Lesson

A brief explanation of the theme is given with corresponding scriptures and discussion questions.

Activity

The activities are meant to reinforce what is taught in the lesson, so they may not be the games your family is used to playing. Many lessons include separate activities for younger children and older children. Generally, the activities for younger children are for ages three to seven, and those activities for older children, eight to eleven. However, don't use this guideline as a firm rule. Some younger children may be advanced for their age, and some older children may still enjoy the activities for younger children.

Activity Printouts

You can download and print the activities at primaryhelper.com/downloads.

Challenge

The challenge should be completed during the week before the next Monday. At the beginning of each family home evening, follow up with your children on the previous week's challenge. Discuss their successes and help them with any problems or concerns.

JANUARY

Heavenly Father Prepared a Way for Me to Return to His Presence

WEEK 1

I am a child of God and can be like Him someday.

Resources

Children's Songbook
I Am a Child of God (2)
My Heavenly Father Loves Me (228)

Hymns
O My Father (292)
I Know My Father Lives (302)

Scriptures
Psalm 82:6
Galatians 4:7

Lesson

Before we came to earth, we lived as spirits with Heavenly Father. He knew and loved us very much, just as He does now. He is the father of our spirits. That means we are literally children of God. Although we have parents here on earth, Heavenly Father will always be the father of our spirits. We cannot see Him, but He will always look out for us, just as our earthly parents do. He wants us to be happy and return to Him someday. He wants to bless us and give us all the wonderful things He has.

Heavenly Father sent us here to earth so we could become more like Him. When we came to earth, we received a body of flesh and bone like His. Here on Earth we can learn the difference between right and wrong and choose the right. Because we are children of God, He wants us to return to Him someday. If we do our best to keep the commandments, we can live with Him again.

Read and discuss Romans 8:16–17.
What is an heir? What does it mean to be joint-heirs with Christ?
Why does Heavenly Father want to share His glory with us?

Activity

Younger Children: Draw a picture of yourself in the picture frame on page 4. You can download and print the activity at primaryhelper.com/downloads.

Older Children: See page 5. You can download and print the activity at primaryhelper.com/downloads.

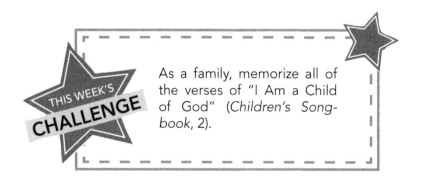

THIS WEEK'S CHALLENGE

As a family, memorize all of the verses of "I Am a Child of God" (*Children's Song-book*, 2).

WORD SEARCH

Below is an excerpt from the New Testament (Romans 8:16–17). Find the words in bold in the word search. Remember, words may appear forward, backward, horizontally, vertically, or diagonally. *Solution on page 145.*

```
A  S  J  Z  O  N  R  I  G  O  D  L  M
H  I  G  L  O  R  I  F  I  E  D  Q  R
Z  B  C  X  W  D  A  H  B  E  I  C  F
C  G  S  P  I  R  I  T  D  J  H  E  I
H  K  J  F  T  M  K  I  G  A  H  I  L
R  A  M  H  N  N  J  O  P  N  K  Q  R
I  S  L  O  E  B  T  J  E  M  U  L  V
S  C  E  Q  S  N  D  R  K  W  O  T  X
T  P  Y  N  S  Z  D  A  R  Q  R  B  C
D  F  P  E  S  L  C  F  T  G  U  F  H
I  V  J  A  I  W  X  K  X  Z  L  Y  M
N  Z  O  H  A  P  B  Q  S  R  I  E  H
R  S  C  D  G  T  D  E  U  F  V  G  W
```

THE **SPIRIT** ITSELF BEARETH **WITNESS** WITH OUR SPIRIT, THAT WE ARE THE **CHILDREN** OF **GOD**:
AND IF CHILDREN, THEN **HEIRS**; HEIRS OF GOD, AND JOINT-HEIRS WITH **CHRIST**; IF SO BE THAT WE SUFFER WITH HIM, THAT WE MAY BE ALSO **GLORIFIED** TOGETHER.

WEEK 2

Heavenly Father provided a Savior so I can return to His presence.

Resources

Children's Songbook
He Sent His Son (34)
Beautiful Savior (62)

Hymns
Redeemer of Israel (6)
The Lord Is My Shepherd (108)

Gospel Art Book
Christ's Image (1)

Scriptures
1 John 4:14
D&C 43:34

Lesson

When Heavenly Father presented the plan of salvation to us, we were excited and shouted with joy. But we knew, and Heavenly Father knew, we could not complete our life on earth alone. No matter how hard we tried to keep the commandments, we would still make mistakes. We needed a Savior—someone who would save us from our sins.

Jesus Christ and Lucifer both volunteered to be our Savior. Lucifer wanted to force us to keep all the commandments, and he wanted to receive all the glory for it. Jesus, on the other hand, said He would let us grow by making our own choices. He would give His life for us in order to redeem us from our sins, and the glory would be His Father's. Heavenly Father chose Jesus to be our Savior and Redeemer.

Because Jesus gave His life for us, we have the freedom to choose right from wrong. When we make a mistake, we can repent and be forgiven. And if we have done that, someday we can return to live with Heavenly Father and Jesus forever. Jesus died for all the world, but He also died for you and me. He knows and loves us each individually. Because of this, you can say that Jesus is your personal Savior and Redeemer.

Read and discuss D&C 93:8–9.
What is the Word?
Why is Jesus called "the light and the Redeemer of the world"?

Activity

All Ages: Watch a video of the Savior. Many beautiful depictions of the Savior can be found at lds.org.

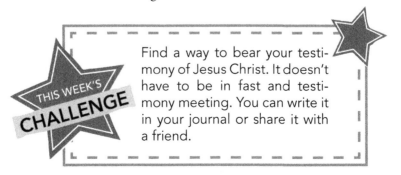

THIS WEEK'S CHALLENGE

Find a way to bear your testimony of Jesus Christ. It doesn't have to be in fast and testimony meeting. You can write it in your journal or share it with a friend.

WEEK 3

Jesus Christ is the perfect example for me to follow.

Resources

Children's Songbook
I'm Trying to Be like Jesus (78)
Love One Another (136)

Hymns
The Lord Is My Light (89)
More Holiness Give Me (131)

Gospel Art Book
Christ's Image (1)
Christ with Children (116)

Scriptures
Matthew 4:19
John 13:15

Lesson

Jesus Christ is the perfect example of how to live because He lived a perfect life. He always obeyed Heavenly Father. He was kind and showed love to everyone, always putting others' needs before His own. When He visited the Nephites, He told them it was time for Him to leave. But then He noticed how much they still needed Him, and He decided to stay. He told them, "Behold my bowels are filled with compassion towards you" (3 Nephi 17:6). Then He invited anyone who was sick or afflicted to come to Him for a blessing. It did not matter to Him that He had planned on leaving and now had to stay longer. He loved these people and wanted to heal them.

If we follow Jesus's example, we will love and serve one another. We will have a greater desire to keep the commandments, and we will grow closer to Heavenly Father and Jesus Christ.

Read and discuss 3 Nephi 27:27.
To whom is Jesus speaking? Does this commandment apply to us as well? Why did Jesus give this commandment?
What are you already doing to become like Jesus? What can you do better?

Activity

Younger Children: See page 10. You can download and print the activity at primaryhelper.com/downloads.
Older Children: See page 11. You can download and print the activity at primaryhelper.com/downloads.

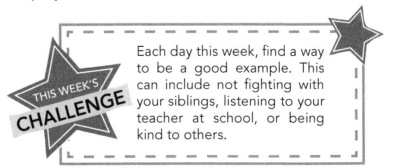

THIS WEEK'S CHALLENGE

Each day this week, find a way to be a good example. This can include not fighting with your siblings, listening to your teacher at school, or being kind to others.

I Follow Jesus Christ by Helping Others

SHAPE SCRAMBLE

Complete the sentence below by matching each shape with a shape in the shape key. Write the matching letter on the blank inside the white shape.
Solution on page 145.

Jesus Christ is the perfect _____ for me to follow.

WEEK 4

I can return to Heavenly Father by following Jesus.

Resources

Children's Songbook
I Feel My Savior's Love (74)
I'm Trying to Be like Jesus (78)

Hymns
The Lord Is My Light (89)
Come, Follow Me (116)

Gospel Art Book
The Sermon on the Mount (39)
Lord, Save Me (43)

Scriptures
Psalm 25:4
Matthew 8:18–22

Lesson

Jesus said, "I am the way, the truth, and the life: no man cometh unto the Father, but by me" (John 14:6). Without Jesus Christ, we cannot return to Heavenly Father. Jesus set the perfect example for us, and we need to follow Him and keep the commandments. We need to love others as He did and serve people without expecting anything in return.

However, we will all fall short. We will all make mistakes and break the commandments. Because Jesus loves us, He died for us so that we can repent and be forgiven of our sins.

If we do our best to follow Jesus Christ, and repent when we do wrong, He will lead us back to Heavenly Father.

Read and discuss 2 Nephi 31:10.
How do we follow Jesus Christ?
Can we follow Him if we disobey the commandments?

Activity

All Ages: Play the game on page 14. Be sure to print and download the activity at primaryhelper.com/downloads. The game board on page 14 is just a sample and is too small to play on.

THIS WEEK'S CHALLENGE

With your family, talk about attributes of the Savior you would like to master. Pick one and strive to develop it this week.

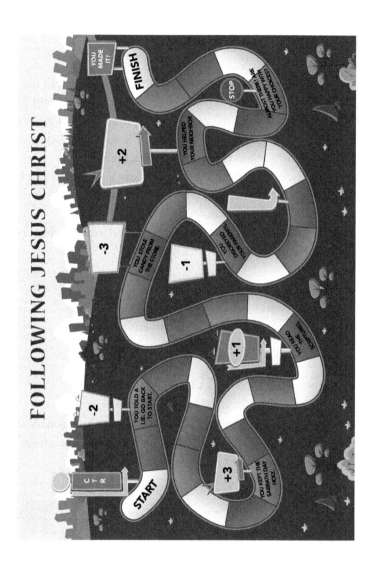

Materials
1 dice

1 pawn for each player (You can use beans, coins, small pieces of candy, or any small objects that fit on the board.)

Rules
1. Take turns rolling the dice.
2. If you land on a space with a negative number, you made a wrong choice and have to go back that number of spaces. If you land on a space with a positive number, you made a good choice and can move forward that number of spaces.
3. The person to reach the finish line first wins.

FEBRUARY

Heavenly Father
Has a Plan for
His Children

WEEK 1

Heavenly Father has a plan for His children.

Resources

Children's Songbook
I Am a Child of God (2)
I Lived in Heaven (4)

Hymns
O My Father (292)
I Am a Child of God (301)

Gospel Art Book
The Earth (3)

Scriptures
Alma 42:13
Moses 6:62

Lesson

Heavenly Father loves us very much. He wants us to feel joy and to have everything that He has. But when we lived with Him as spirits in the premortal world, we did not have bodies like He has. And because we had always lived with Him, we hadn't experienced certain things that would help us to grow.

Heavenly Father created a plan for each of us. It is called the plan of salvation. Through this plan we all chose to come to earth and gain a physical body. We chose to follow Jesus Christ and keep the commandments. If we do this, we will return to live with Heavenly Father after we die. We will have great joy because we will have become like Him.

Read and discuss Moses 1:39.
What is God's "work and glory"?
What does it mean to "bring to pass the immortality and eternal life of man"?

Activity

All Ages: Play a game of kickball or baseball. Have each base represent a step in the plan of salvation (first base: earth life, second base: death, third base: the spirit world, home plate: final judgment/celestial kingdom). Explain to your children that just like in life, there will be obstacles and challenges in this game. The opposing team will try to get you out, and you must do all you can to make it to safety.

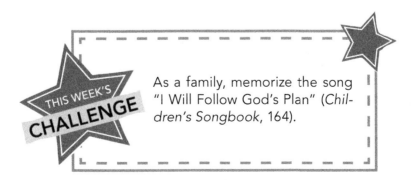

THIS WEEK'S CHALLENGE

As a family, memorize the song "I Will Follow God's Plan" (*Children's Songbook*, 164).

WEEK 2

Heavenly Father commanded Jesus Christ to create the earth.

Resources

Children's Songbook
My Heavenly Father Loves Me (228)
All Things Bright and Beautiful (231)

Hymns
All Creatures of Our God and King (62)
For the Beauty of the Earth (92)

Gospel Art Book
The Lord Created All Things (2)
The Earth (3)

Scriptures
John 1:10
Colossians 1:16

Lesson

As part of the plan of happiness, we needed a place where we could receive a physical body and be tested. Jesus Christ created the earth under the direction of Heavenly Father. We are here on earth to learn and grow and take care of our physical bodies.

Jesus Christ created many wonderful things for us to enjoy here on earth. Let's read about the creation of the earth in Genesis chapter 1.

Read and discuss Genesis 1.
What did Jesus create first? Last?
Why did He rest on the seventh day?

Activity

Younger Children: See page 20. You can download and print the activity at primaryhelper.com/downloads.
Older Children: See page 21. You can download and print the activity at primaryhelper.com/downloads.

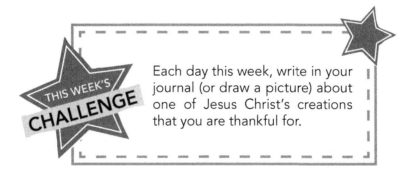

THIS WEEK'S CHALLENGE

Each day this week, write in your journal (or draw a picture) about one of Jesus Christ's creations that you are thankful for.

Cut out each card and play a matching game with the duplicate pairs.

EARTH SCRAMBLE

Unscramble the words in the pictures below to discover what Jesus created on what day. *Solution on page 145.*

DAY 1
YAD, GHINT

DAY 2
ULODCS, CNOSEA

DAY 3
NALD, STANPL, RESET

DAY 4
UNS, NOMO, SRATS

DAY 5
SHIF, RIDBS, ANALMSI

DAY 6
ANM

DAY 1: _____

DAY 2: _____

DAY 3: _____

DAY 4: _____

DAY 5: _____

DAY 6: _____

WEEK 3

My body is created in the image of God.

Resources

Children's Songbook
I Am a Child of God (2)
The Lord Gave Me a Temple (153)

Hymns
Sweet Is the Peace the Gospel Brings (14)
Keep the Commandments (303)

Gospel Art Book
Young Boy Praying (111)
Christ with Children (116)

Scriptures
Mosiah 2:37
Ether 3:16

Lesson

Before we came to earth, we lived in heaven with our Heavenly Father. We were His spirit children. Heavenly Father wanted us to have a physical body like His so that we could become more like Him. He and Jesus Christ created the earth so that we would have a place to receive a body. In the Old Testament we learn that "God created man in his own image, in the image of God created he him; male and female created he them" (Genesis 1:27). Heavenly Father created us to look like Him. He has a body of flesh and bone, just as we do. He has a head and arms and legs and a face just like we do. The Prophet Joseph Smith testified of this when Heavenly Father and Jesus Christ appeared to him in the Sacred Grove. Joseph Smith said that he saw two personages and that they were men similar to us.

Our bodies are a sacred gift from Heavenly Father. We need to show respect to them and take good care of them. How can you take good care of your body?

Read and discuss Doctrine and Covenants 130:22.
What is God's body made of?
How is your body like Heavenly Father's?

Activity

Younger Children: See page 24. Color or decorate the outline of the body so that it looks like yours. You can download and print the activity at primaryhelper.com/downloads.
Older Children: See page 25. You can download and print the activity at primaryhelper.com/downloads.

THIS WEEK'S CHALLENGE

One of the ways we can take care of our bodies is to keep them active. Do three things to keep your body active: go for a walk, play a game of soccer, ride your bike, and so on.

BODY IMAGES

This boy is taking care of his body. Find three differences in each duplicate pair of pictures. *Solution on page 145.*

WEEK 4

Agency is the gift to choose for myself.

Resources

Children's Songbook
Nephi's Courage (120)
Dare to Do Right (158)

Hymns
Choose the Right (239)
Teach Me to Walk in the Light (304)

Gospel Art Book
Adam and Eve Teaching Their Children (5)
Family Prayer (112)

Scriptures
D&C 101:78
Articles of Faith 1:2

Lesson

In the scriptures we read that men are "agents unto themselves" (Moses 6:56). That means each of us can make choices for ourselves. No one can force us to do anything against our will.

Before we came to earth, there was a great war in heaven. When Heavenly Father presented the plan of happiness, He told us that we would need to make good choices in order to return to Him. But Heavenly Father knew it would not be easy and that we would need a savior. Lucifer said that he would be our savior and force us to keep the commandments so we could return to Heavenly Father. But that was not a good plan because we wouldn't have the freedom to choose. Jesus Christ said He would be our savior and teach us the right way. Then we would each decide which path to take. Heavenly Father was pleased with this plan because He wanted us to have agency, or the freedom to choose for ourselves. We chose to come to earth and follow Jesus Christ.

Here on earth we are faced with choices each day. We have the freedom to choose between right and wrong, and we will be responsible for our choices. If we choose the right, we will be blessed. If we choose to sin, we will have to suffer the consequences.

Read and discuss Helaman 14:29–31.
What happens if we make good choices?
What happens if we choose evil?

Activity

All Ages: Fill a large suitcase or a garbage bag with various items of clothing. Ask a child to close his eyes and choose three items of clothing from the bag. No matter what he chooses, tell him it is the outfit he has to wear the next day. Ask him how he feels about not getting a choice. Discuss the importance of agency and reiterate that it is a great gift from Heavenly Father.

NOTE: See page 28 for this week's challenge.

THIS WEEK'S CHALLENGE

Each time before you make a decision this week, stop and ask yourself if it is a good or bad choice. Ask yourself if the decision will help you grow closer to the Savior.

MARCH

Jesus Christ Is Our Savior

WEEK 1

I can gain a testimony of Jesus Christ.

Resources

Children's Songbook
Jesus Has Risen (70)
Search, Ponder, and Pray (109)

Hymns
I Know That My Redeemer Lives (136)
Testimony (137)

Gospel Art Book
Living Water (36)
Go Ye Therefore, and Teach
    All Nations (61)

Scriptures
Psalm 19:7, D&C 76:22

Lesson

One day Jesus asked His Apostle Peter who he thought Jesus was. Peter answered, "Thou art the Christ, the Son of the living God" (Matthew 16:16).

Jesus replied, "Blessed art thou . . . for flesh and blood hath not revealed it unto thee, but my Father which is in heaven" (Matthew 16:17).

Peter had a testimony that Jesus was the Christ. He did not know this because anyone on earth had told him. He knew this because the Holy Ghost had borne witness to him.

Heavenly Father wants us all to have our own testimony of Jesus Christ. That means He wants us all to know for ourselves that Jesus Christ is our Savior. Someone can tell us that Jesus Christ is our Savior, but we have to believe it and know it for ourselves. We each must have our own witness from the Holy Ghost that Jesus Christ lives.

Gaining a testimony can be a slow a process. It doesn't happen overnight. We have to go to church, read the scriptures, and pray before we can gain a testimony. When we do these things, we will feel peace from the Holy Ghost, and our testimony will grow.

Read and discuss Alma 7:13.
What was Alma's testimony?
How can you develop a testimony of the Savior?

Activity

All Ages: Write down your testimony of the Savior and send it to a friend or relative in a letter. Explain why Jesus Christ is important to you. If you don't know how to write yet, you can draw a picture and have a parent help you.

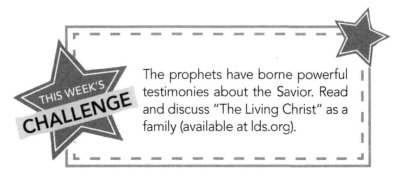

THIS WEEK'S CHALLENGE

The prophets have borne powerful testimonies about the Savior. Read and discuss "The Living Christ" as a family (available at lds.org).

WEEK 2

Through the Atonement I can repent and be forgiven of my sins.

Resources

Children's Songbook
He Sent His Son (34)
He Died That We Might Live Again (65)

Hymns
I Know That My Redeemer Lives (136)
Jesus, Once of Humble Birth (196)

Gospel Art Book
Christ in Gethsemane (56)
The Crucifixion (57)

Scriptures
John 3:16
Helaman 5:9

Lesson

Heavenly Father knew we would make mistakes when we came to earth. That's why He provided a Savior for us. Jesus Christ died for us so that we can live with Heavenly Father again. This is called the Atonement.

When Jesus was in the Garden of Gethsemane, He suffered for all of our sins. He paid the price of our sins so that we won't have to if we repent. Then He died on the cross, giving Himself as a sacrifice for all mankind. His body was placed to rest in a tomb. On the third day, He was resurrected. His spirit and body were reunited. He is alive again and will never be able to die again.

Because of Christ's great gift to us, we will be resurrected someday. But more important, we can repent and be cleansed from our sins. The Atonement of Jesus Christ makes it possible to live with Heavenly Father again.

Read and discuss Helaman 5:9.
How did Jesus Christ redeem the world?
Why is He the only way back to our Heavenly Father?

Activity

All Ages: Fill a jar with water and tell your children that the water represents their spirit. Then add a couple drops of food coloring, which represents sin. Stir the water until the food coloring dyes all of the water. Explain that when we sin, our spirits get "dirty." Add some bleach to the jar and watch the color disappear. Explain that through the Atonement, we can be washed clean from our sins.

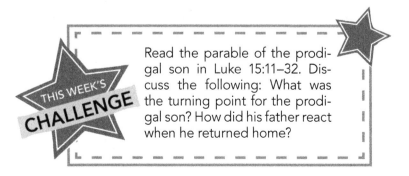

THIS WEEK'S CHALLENGE

Read the parable of the prodigal son in Luke 15:11–32. Discuss the following: What was the turning point for the prodigal son? How did his father react when he returned home?

WEEK 3

Jesus Christ was resurrected, and I will be too.

Resources

Children's Songbook
Did Jesus Really Live Again? (64)
The Lord Gave Me a Temple (153)

Hymns
My Redeemer Lives (135)
He Is Risen! (199)

Gospel Art Book
Why Weepest Thou? (59)
Behold My Hands and Feet (60)

Scriptures
Matthew 28:6
Alma 40:23

Lesson

When Jesus Christ died on the cross for us, His body was placed in a tomb. On the third day, when His disciples went to check on Him, they found His tomb empty. Jesus had overcome death and had been resurrected. His spirit and His body were reunited.

Through the Atonement of Jesus Christ, we too will be resurrected. Our spirits and our bodies will come together again and be perfected. We will no longer suffer illness or injury. For example, a blind man will be able to see again. A deaf man will hear again. Someone who lost a leg in this life will be able to walk and run perfectly. Resurrection is a gift to everyone on this earth because Heavenly Father and Jesus love us so much.

Read and discuss Mosiah 16:6–9.
How is death "swallowed up in Christ"?
Why does "the grave [have] no victory"?
In verse 9 we read that "there can be no more death." Does this mean that
   since Christ was resurrected no one can die anymore?

Activity

All Ages, Option 1: Visit the grave of a family member or friend and take flowers to decorate it. While you are there, discuss what you learned in this lesson.

All Ages, Option 2: Look at pictures of your ancestors or others who have passed away. Who are you excited to see again? Talk about what you will say to them when you see them again.

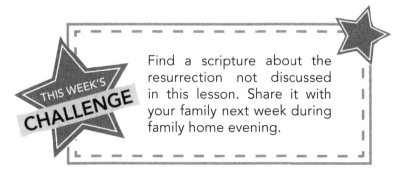

THIS WEEK'S CHALLENGE

Find a scripture about the resurrection not discussed in this lesson. Share it with your family next week during family home evening.

WEEK 4

I can show respect for the Savior by being reverent.

Resources

Children's Songbook
Reverently, Quietly (26)
I Want to Be Reverent (28)

Hymns
Oh, May My Soul Commune with Thee (123)
Reverently and Meekly Now (185)

Gospel Art Book
Passing the Sacrament (108)
Young Boy Praying (111)

Scriptures
Psalm 89:7
D&C 107:4

Lesson

Imagine your family is having fun playing a board game at the kitchen table. Your friend walks in the front door, comes over to the table, and throws the game and the pieces on the floor. Then he starts yelling at everyone and ruins your perfect evening. How would you feel? What would you do? Most likely, you would be very upset and ask him why he did that. You might explain to him that your family was enjoying time together and that he disrupted it. You might also explain to your friend that your feelings are hurt because he did not respect you and your family.

Jesus Christ feels the same way when we are not reverent at church. Being reverent means sitting quietly and listening. It means keeping our hands still and not making noise. By being reverent, we show our love and respect for Jesus. When we are not reverent, our actions tell Him that we don't love Him enough to quietly listen to the lesson. We show Him that talking to a friend or misbehaving is more important than His gospel.

What can you do this week to show reverence?

Read and discuss Hebrews 12:28.
What is reverence? What is godly fear?
How can we show reverence and godly fear for God?

Activity

All Ages: Play the matching game "More than Just Quietly Sitting" from the October 2016 *Friend* magazine. You can download and print the game at media.ldscdn.org/pdf/magazines/friend-october-2016/2016 -10-13-happy-sabbath-more-than-just-quietly-sitting-eng.pdf.

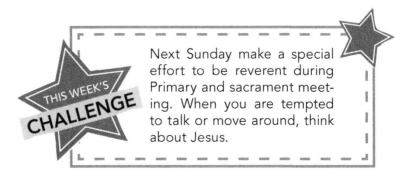

THIS WEEK'S CHALLENGE

Next Sunday make a special effort to be reverent during Primary and sacrament meeting. When you are tempted to talk or move around, think about Jesus.

APRIL

The Family Is Central to God's Plan

WEEK 1

The family is central to God's plan.

Resources

Children's Songbook
The Hearts of the Children (92)
I Love to See the Temple (95)

Hymns
Home Can Be a Heaven on Earth (298)
Families Can Be Together Forever (300)

Gospel Art Book
Adam and Eve Teaching Their Children (5)
Family Prayer (112)

Scriptures
Malachi 4:6
D&C 138:48

Lesson

What would your life be like without your family? It would get pretty lonely, wouldn't it? And it would be pretty scary at times. We need families for many reasons. Families take care of each other and give each other support. Most important, families are central to Heavenly Father's plan.

From the beginning of time, families have lived on the earth. Adam and Eve were the first family. They were commanded to have children and found much joy as their family grew. Another righteous family in the scriptures is Lehi and Sariah's family in the Book of Mormon. God commanded Lehi to take his family into the wilderness and start a new life. Jerusalem, the city where they lived, was full of wicked people and was about to be destroyed. God wanted to save this family because they were righteous. Even though Laman and Lemuel complained a lot, they went with their family. The family had many trials during their journey, but they worked together to fulfill God's plan.

Read and discuss 1 Nephi 2:4.

What did Lehi and his family leave behind? What did they take with them? Imagine your family had to do something similar and that you didn't have anything left except each other. Name one strength that each member of your family has that would help your family survive.

Activity

Younger Children: On page 42 you'll find a picture of an empty temple. Draw a picture of your family in the temple. You can download and print the activity at primaryhelper.com/downloads.

Older Children: See page 43. You can download and print the activity at primaryhelper.com/downloads.

THIS WEEK'S CHALLENGE

Show someone in your family how much you love them. You could help your parents with extra chores or share your toys with your siblings.

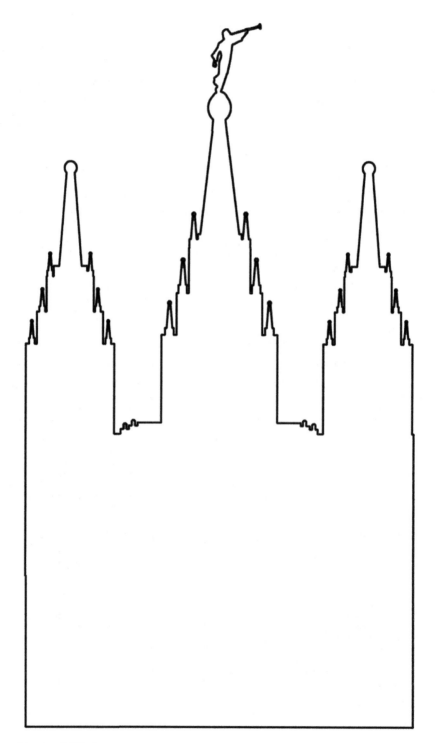

FAMILY SEARCH

Find the names of different family members in the word search. Remember, words may appear forward, backward, horizontally, vertically, or diagonally. *Solution on page 145.*

```
N  A  N  B  M  B  F  D  S  C  G  O  D
I  E  G  R  A  N  D  M  A  F  R  M  E
E  G  M  O  M  G  H  A  U  E  A  I  O
C  P  A  T  B  B  A  K  N  H  N  O  N
E  A  K  H  C  I  C  F  T  U  D  B  E
C  R  H  E  J  H  D  R  C  K  P  L  P
E  F  M  R  G  L  Q  N  B  H  A  O  H
C  O  U  S  I  N  P  R  I  D  L  J  E
K  S  Q  D  U  L  I  V  E  R  A  M  W
F  S  N  D  A  D  T  G  O  T  P  U  G
C  Q  E  H  R  V  U  G  W  K  S  I  X
Q  T  W  Z  B  C  S  B  U  G  R  I  L
E  L  C  N  U  M  R  T  Q  X  C  B  S
```

MOM	AUNT
DAD	UNCLE
BROTHER	COUSIN
SISTER	NIECE
GRANDMA	NEPHEW
GRANDPA	

WEEK 2

Parents have important responsibilities in families.

Resources

Children's Songbook
My Mother Dear (203)
Fathers (209)

Hymns
O My Father (292)
Teach Me to Walk in the Light (304)

Gospel Art Book
Adam and Eve Teaching Their
    Children (5)

Scriptures
Moroni 8:10
Moses 6:54

Lesson

Why do you think Heavenly Father gave you parents? Was it so that you had someone to boss you around and make you do your chores? Or did He provide us each with parents so we have loving adults to protect us and help us learn and grow?

The prophets have taught that being a parent is a sacred responsibility. Parents are raising Heavenly Father's spirit children. They need to provide food, shelter, clothing, and other necessities for their children. But more important, they need to provide a loving home where the Holy Ghost can dwell, and where the children can learn about Jesus Christ. Parents need to set a good example and teach their children how to pray and study the scriptures. When we see how much our parents love us, we can better understand how much Heavenly Father loves us.

Read and discuss Mosiah 4:14–15.
What are parents' responsibilities?
How can you help your parents fulfill their responsibilities?

Activity

Younger Children: Go on a picture scavenger hunt. Look for pictures in magazines or books that show parents and their children. The first person to find five pictures wins.

Older Children: Go on a scripture scavenger hunt. Look for scriptures that talk about parents' responsibilities. The first person to find five scriptures wins.

THIS WEEK'S CHALLENGE

Show your parents how much you appreciate them. Draw them a picture, write them a note, or do an act of service for them.

WEEK 3

Children have the responsibility to obey their parents.

Resources

Children's Songbook
Love Is Spoken Here (190)
The Family (194)

Hymns
Home Can Be a Heaven on Earth (298)
Teach Me to Walk in the Light (304)

Gospel Art Book
Family Prayer (112)

Scriptures
Proverbs 4:1
Colossians 3:20

Lesson

All members of a family have great responsibilities. Last week we talked about parents' responsibilities. What do you think your responsibilities are as a child?

One of the Ten Commandments states, "Honour thy father and thy mother" (Exodus 20:12). That means you should show your parents respect and obey them. All parents have rules, and sometimes they have to give consequences when we don't follow them. But they only do that because they love us. They want us to be obedient and keep the commandments so our family can be together forever.

When children obey their parents, there is love and harmony in the home. It is easier to feel the Spirit and follow Jesus Christ.

Read and discuss Ephesians 6:1.
What does it mean to "obey your parents in the Lord"?
How do you think your parents feel when you disobey them?

Activity

All Ages: This week let your parents choose an activity that they'd like to do as a family. It may not be something you enjoy, but respect your parents' wishes and try to have a good time.

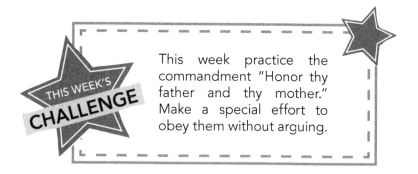

THIS WEEK'S CHALLENGE

This week practice the commandment "Honor thy father and thy mother." Make a special effort to obey them without arguing.

WEEK 4

I can show love to each member of my family.

Resources

Children's Songbook
Jesus Said Love Everyone (61)
Love One Another (136)

Hymns
Each Life That Touches Ours for
    Good (293)
Love at Home (294)

Scriptures
1 John 4:20
Moroni 7:47

Lesson

Our families are one of the greatest gifts our Heavenly Father has given us. Without them we would be lost and very lonely. As with all precious gifts, we need to treasure it and strengthen our family relationships.

We can show our love for our family members in many different ways. In addition to saying, "I love you," or giving a hug, we can show our family that we love them by doing these simple things:

- obeying our parents
- serving each other
- sharing with our siblings
- including everyone when we're playing a game
- reading to a younger sibling
- writing notes or drawing pictures for each other

There are countless ways to show love for each other. How do you show yours?

Read and discuss John 13:34–35.
What commandment did Jesus give His disciples?
How can we show our love to each other?

Activity

All Ages: Put each family member's name in a paper bag. Take turns drawing a name. When each name is drawn, take turns saying something nice about that person.

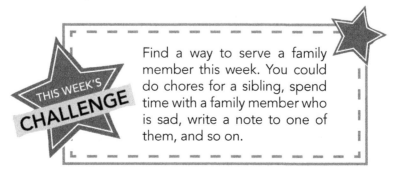

THIS WEEK'S CHALLENGE

Find a way to serve a family member this week. You could do chores for a sibling, spend time with a family member who is sad, write a note to one of them, and so on.

MAY

Families Are Blessed When They Follow the Prophet

WEEK 1

God speaks to us through prophets.

Resources

Children's Songbook
Seek the Lord Early (108)
The Seventh Article of Faith (126)

Hymns
The Voice of God Again Is Heard (18)
Hark, All Ye Nations! (264)

Scriptures
1 Nephi 22:1–2
D&C 43:1–7

Lesson

The prophet is often called the Lord's mouthpiece because he tells us the mind and will of the Lord. He tells us what God would tell us if He were here.

Moses told Pharaoh to free the children of Israel. Lehi commanded the people of Jerusalem to repent. Today we are led by living prophets. Russell M. Nelson is the President of the Church. He has two counselors and twelve Apostles. All of these men are considered prophets. They teach us what Jesus would teach us if He were here with us. The prophets have told us to repent of our sins, hold family home evening, read the scriptures, pray daily, and many other things that will help us become closer to Heavenly Father and Jesus Christ. We learn in the Doctrine and Covenants that when the prophet speaks, he is speaking for Heavenly Father. Let's read that verse.

Read and discuss D&C 1:38.
Why does God speak through prophets?
How should we treat the prophets' words?

Activity

All Ages: Go to lds.org/church/leaders. Look at the pictures of the First Presidency and members of the Quorum of the Twelve Apostles. How many do you recognize? Click on their pictures to learn more about them.

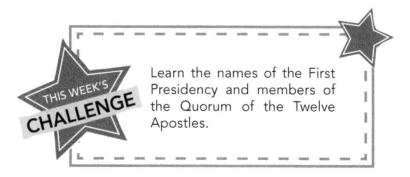

THIS WEEK'S CHALLENGE

Learn the names of the First Presidency and members of the Quorum of the Twelve Apostles.

WEEK 2

The prophets in the scriptures are examples to my family.

Lesson

In the Old Testament we read of a prophet named Abraham. He and his wife, Sariah, wanted a child very much, but Sariah was not able to have children. After many years, when Abraham and Sariah were both old, Sariah gave birth to a boy named Isaac. It was a miracle! Abraham and Sariah felt great joy and were very grateful to Heavenly Father.

When Isaac was older, God commanded Abraham to take Isaac up a mountain and sacrifice him. Abraham didn't want to. He loved Isaac very much. But he also trusted God and wanted to obey Him.

Abraham took Isaac up a mountain and built an altar. He laid his son on the altar and was ready to sacrifice him. An angel appeared to him and stopped him, saying that God was only testing Abraham.

Abraham is a great example of obedience. God asked him to do something very, very hard, and he was willing, even though it made him very sad. If we are obedient like Abraham was, we will be greatly blessed.

Read and discuss Genesis 22:15–18.
How was Abraham blessed for being obedient to the Lord?
What blessings will our family receive if we are obedient?

Activity

All Ages: Play a game of charades and act out different stories found in the scriptures. You can use the following ideas or come up with your own: Noah, Moses, King Benjamin, Alma, Nephi, Moroni.

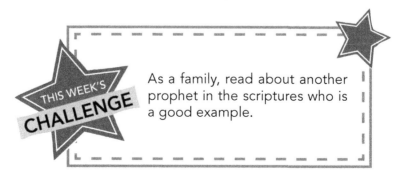

THIS WEEK'S CHALLENGE

As a family, read about another prophet in the scriptures who is a good example.

WEEK 3

My family will be blessed as we follow the prophet.

Resources

Children's Songbook
Follow the Prophet (110)
Nephi's Courage (120)

Hymns
We Ever Pray for Thee (23)
Praise to the Man (27)

Gospel Art Book
Moses and the Tablets (14)

Scriptures
2 Nephi 9:48
D&C 78:18

Lesson

When Nephi and his family were searching for the promised land, the Lord told them, "Inasmuch as ye shall keep my commandments ye shall prosper in the land; but inasmuch as ye will not keep my commandments ye shall be cut off from my presence" (2 Nephi 1:20). The same promise applies to each of us. When we follow the prophet, Heavenly Father will bless us.

[Tell your children about some of the blessings you have received for following the prophet. Be as specific as possible and use terms they can understand. Then ask them how they have been blessed by following the prophet.]

Read and discuss Doctrine and Covenants 82:10.
Why is the Lord bound when we do what He says?
What does it mean to "have no promise"?

Activity

All Ages: Organize a commandments treasure hunt for your children, hiding each clue in a place that relates to counsel from the prophet. Older children should help the younger ones figure out the clues. Place a treat or another reward at the end of the hunt. Explain to your children the correlation between the treasure hunt and how we are blessed for keeping the commandments. Use the following clues or come up with your own:

- No other gods before me (hide the clue near a picture of the Savior)
- Keep the Sabbath day holy (near a calendar or someone's church shoes)
- Honor thy father and mother (in parents' room or on their bed)
- Pay your tithing (near a piggy bank)
- Keep the Word of Wisdom (on the refrigerator)
- Dress modestly (in someone's closet or dresser)

THIS WEEK'S CHALLENGE

Memorize the song "Follow the Prophet" (*Children's Songbook*, 110).

WEEK 4

The prophet speaks to us at general conference.

Resources

Children's Songbook
The Sixth Article of Faith (126)
Latter-day Prophets (134)

Hymns
We Thank Thee, O God, for a
   Prophet (19)
God Bless Our Prophet Dear (24)

Scriptures
D&C 1:38
Articles of Faith 1:6

Lesson

April and October are important months. On the first weekend of these months, we get to listen to the prophets and apostles speak to us in general conference. They pray beforehand to know what Heavenly Father wants them to say. Because of this, they are speaking for Heavenly Father.

General conference takes place in Salt Lake City at the Conference Center on Temple Square. Thousands of people go there to listen to the prophets and apostles. But there are many people in the world, and not everyone can go to Salt Lake City. Those of us who don't attend general conference in person can watch it on television or on the Internet. We can even listen to it on the radio. No matter where we live, we can listen to the prophets and apostles speak, and we can hear the word of God.

Read and discuss Amos 3:7.

What are some of the things the prophet and apostles have taught recently in general conference?

How can we hear conference talks if we can't go to Salt Lake City?

Activity

All Ages: As a family, read or watch a conference talk. Make a poster with words or pictures that represent the talk. Hang it in the dining room or another prominent place where you will see it often and be reminded of the prophet's words.

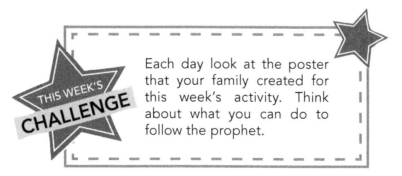

THIS WEEK'S CHALLENGE

Each day look at the poster that your family created for this week's activity. Think about what you can do to follow the prophet.

JUNE

Priesthood Ordinances
and Temple Work
Bless My Family

WEEK 1

Priesthood ordinances bless and strengthen my family.

Resources

Children's Songbook
The Priesthood Is Restored (89)
The Fifth Article of Faith (125)

Hymns
Praise to the Man (27)
Hark, All Ye Nations! (264)

Gospel Art Book
Young Man Being Baptized (103)
Salt Lake Temple (119)

Scriptures
3 Nephi 11:21
D&C 68:8

Lesson

Priesthood ordinances bless and strengthen our family. Ordinances include taking the sacrament, being baptized, receiving the gift of the Holy Ghost, and being endowed in the temple. All of these ordinances prepare us for the greatest ordinance of all: being sealed to our family for time and all eternity.

When we receive these priesthood ordinances, we make sacred covenants with Heavenly Father. We promise to serve Him and keep the commandments. We promise to stand as a witness of Jesus Christ.

The most important priesthood ordinance is being sealed for time and all eternity in the temple. When we are sealed in the temple, we promise to love each other and do all we can to help each other make it back to Heavenly Father.

When we honor our covenants, we have the constant companionship of the Holy Ghost. We have peace in our home, and our love for each other grows.

Read and discuss D&C 136:4.
What is our covenant?
What does it mean to "walk in all the ordinances of the Lord"?

Activity

All Ages: Watch one of the Bible videos on lds.org that shows Jesus using the priesthood. Videos are available at lds.org/media-library/video/categories/bible-videos-the -life-of-jesus-christ?lang=eng.

THIS WEEK'S CHALLENGE

Show your appreciation to a priesthood holder. You could write him a note, make him a treat, draw him a picture, or do something that will make his calling easier this week.

WEEK 2

Temples make it possible for families to be together forever.

Resources

Children's Songbook
The Hearts of the Children (92)
I Love to See the Temple (95)

Hymns
How Beautiful Thy Temples, Lord (288)
Families Can Be Together Forever (300)

Gospel Art Book
Young Couple Going to the Temple (120)
Temple Baptismal Font (121)

Scriptures
D&C 2
D&C 128:15

Lesson

Have you ever thought about what life would be like without your family? Maybe someone in your family has died, or maybe you know someone who has had a family member die. Losing someone you love is very difficult. Heavenly Father understands this, and He doesn't want families to be separated. We may lose our loved ones through death, but Heavenly Father has prepared a way for families to be together again after this life.

Families who are sealed in the temple will be together forever. Husbands and wives will be married forever, and their children will still belong to them after they die. But what about those who die before they get a chance to go to the temple? We can do their temple work for them and seal them to their families. Heavenly Father wants every family who has ever lived or will live on this earth to be an eternal family.

Read and discuss Helaman 10:7.
What does it mean to be sealed in the temple?
Why are temples important to the plan of salvation?

Activity

Younger Children: Do the puzzle on page 66. Print the puzzle from primaryhelper.com, cut out the pieces, and put the puzzle back together.
Older Children: See page 67. You can download and print the activity from primaryhelper.com/downloads.

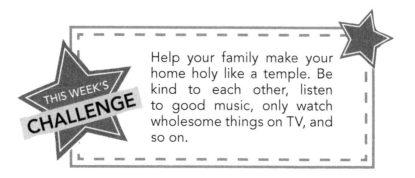

THIS WEEK'S CHALLENGE

Help your family make your home holy like a temple. Be kind to each other, listen to good music, only watch wholesome things on TV, and so on.

I LOVE TO SEE THE TEMPLE

Find seven differences in the temples below. *Solution on page 145.*

WEEK 3

I can prepare now to be worthy to enter the temple.

Resources

Children's Songbook
I Want to Live the Gospel (148)
I Have a Family Tree (199)

Hymns
The Day Dawn Is Breaking (52)
God Is in His Holy Temple (132)

Gospel Art Book
Salt Lake Temple (119)

Scriptures
Psalm 24:3–4
Moroni 10:32

Lesson

The temple is a sacred place. It is the house of God. Because of that, we have to be worthy to enter it. That means we have to be clean spiritually and live the gospel. In addition, we need to be mature enough, or old enough, to understand the ordinances and sacred covenants that we make in the temple.

When Howard W. Hunter was the prophet, he wanted every member of the Church to have a temple recommend, even if they didn't live near a temple. He knew that living worthily would bless their lives, even if they couldn't attend the temple. When you are twelve years old, you can get a limited use recommend and do baptisms for the dead. In the meantime, you can prepare for that day. It is still important to live the gospel so that when you are old enough to go to the temple you don't have to change your habits.

How can we prepare to go to the temple?

Read and discuss Mormon 9:29.
How do we do all things in worthiness?
Why must we be worthy to enter the temple?

Activity

All Ages: Give each child a straw, an empty bowl, and a bowl of M&Ms or Skittles. Give them one minute to suck up the orange candy with the straw and place them in the empty bowl. When they are finished, explain that just as there was a time limit in this game, we have a limited amount of time to prepare to go to the temple. We have been given specific instructions on how to prepare. In this game, the instructions were to place only the orange candy in the bowl. None of the other colors would help them accomplish the goal. Explain that in life we have to make choices, and not all choices will help us get to the temple.

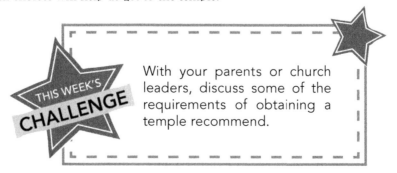

THIS WEEK'S CHALLENGE

With your parents or church leaders, discuss some of the requirements of obtaining a temple recommend.

WEEK 4

Family history work connects me to my ancestors.

Resources

Children's Songbook
Family History—I Am Doing It (94)
Families Can Be Together Forever (188)

Hymns
High on the Mountain Top (5)
We Love Thy House, O God (247)

Gospel Art Book
Nauvoo Illinois Temple (118)
Temple Baptismal Font (121)

Scriptures
Matthew 16:19
1 Peter 3:19

Lesson

The family is central to the plan of salvation. Heavenly Father wants us to be connected not only to our immediate family but also to our extended family and ancestors. How do we connect ourselves to those we have never met who have already passed on?

Family history work provides us with that opportunity. We can do the temple work for our ancestors and be sealed to them. We can also ask our parents and other family members what they remember about our ancestors. Some people are lucky enough to have journals and histories written by their ancestors. They can read about their ancestors' lives and learn about how they gained a testimony or overcame trials.

Some families may not have photos or journals of their ancestors. They can work on preserving memories for their descendants (children, grandchildren, great-grandchildren, and so on). They can collect pictures and write down stories from their lives that their descendants can have someday.

How is your family doing family history?

Read and discuss Malachi 4:6.
Who are the children and who are the fathers in this verse?
How will their hearts be turned to each other?

Activity

All Ages: Complete the family tree on page 72.

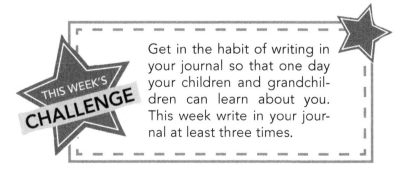

THIS WEEK'S CHALLENGE

Get in the habit of writing in your journal so that one day your children and grandchildren can learn about you. This week write in your journal at least three times.

MY FAMILY TREE

JULY

We Become Members
of the Church
through Baptism
and Confirmation

WEEK 1

The Church of Jesus Christ has been restored.

Resources

Children's Songbook
The Church of Jesus Christ (77)
On a Golden Springtime (88)

Hymns
High on the Mountain Top (5)
Hark, All Ye Nations! (264)

Gospel Art Book
Missionaries: Elders (109)
Missionaries: Sisters (110)

Scriptures
Revelation 14:6
3 Nephi 16:7

Lesson

When Jesus was on the earth, He gave the priesthood keys to His Apostles. That means that after Jesus returned to Heavenly Father, His Apostles had the authority, or power, to act in Jesus's name and continue to lead His Church. But there were many wicked people on the earth who did not want to follow Jesus and belong to His Church. They killed His Apostles, and after they were gone, no one had the authority to lead the Church of Jesus Christ.

For hundreds of years, the Church of Jesus Christ was not on the earth. People still believed in Jesus Christ and formed other churches, but no one had the authority to act for Jesus Christ. None of these churches was the true Church of Jesus Christ.

Thankfully, in 1830, the Church of Jesus Christ was restored through the Prophet Joseph Smith. Joseph Smith translated the Book of Mormon and received all the priesthood keys to lead the Church. Today we have the fulness of the gospel. That means we have the same church that Jesus established when He was on the earth. God has promised that He will never again take the priesthood from the earth.

Read and discuss Doctrine and Covenants 132:45.
What has God restored?
What does God mean when He says He will "make known unto you all things in due time"?

Activity

All Ages: Watch *The Restoration*, available at lds.org/media-library/video/2008-06-01-the-restoration?lang=eng.

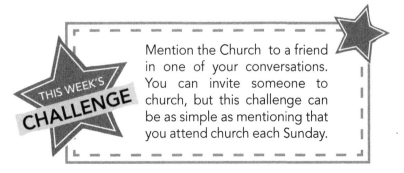

THIS WEEK'S CHALLENGE

Mention the Church to a friend in one of your conversations. You can invite someone to church, but this challenge can be as simple as mentioning that you attend church each Sunday.

WEEK 2

I become a member of the Church through baptism and confirmation.

Resources

Children's Songbook
When Jesus Christ Was Baptized (102)
The Holy Ghost (105)

Hymns
Lead Me into Life Eternal (45)
Lord, Accept into Thy Kingdom (236)

Gospel Art Book
Girl Being Baptized (104)
The Gift of the Holy Ghost (105)

Scriptures
Acts 2:38
3 Nephi 12:2

Lesson

Last week we talked about the Church of Jesus Christ. Heavenly Father wants all of us to become members of the true church. To do so, we must be baptized by a priesthood holder and confirmed a member of the Church.

As soon as you turn eight, you can be baptized. Baptism is an important step that we must take to return to Heavenly Father. When we are baptized, we make sacred covenants with Heavenly Father. We promise Him we will keep His commandments, and He promises to forgive us for our sins.

After we are baptized, a Melchizedek Priesthood holder lays his hands upon our head and confirms us a member of The Church of Jesus Christ of Latter-day Saints. He also gives us the gift of the Holy Ghost. If we keep the commandments and repent when we sin, the Holy Ghost will be our constant companion. He will comfort us, guide us, reveal truth to us, and help us feel the love of Heavenly Father and Jesus Christ.

Read and discuss our baptismal covenants in Mosiah 18:8–10.
What do we promise Heavenly Father when we are baptized?
What does Heavenly Father promise to do for us?

Activity

Younger Children: See page 78. You can download and print the activity at primaryhelper.com/downloads.
Older Children: See page 79. You can download and print the activity at primaryhelper.com/downloads.

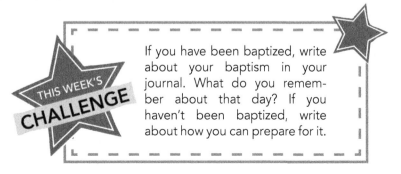

THIS WEEK'S CHALLENGE

If you have been baptized, write about your baptism in your journal. What do you remember about that day? If you haven't been baptized, write about how you can prepare for it.

GREAT TO BE EIGHT

Color all of the squares that have an 8. Then have your parents help you read the message that remains.

8	8	I	8	8	C	8	A	8
N	8	8	B	8	8	E	8	8
8	8	B	8	8	A	8	8	P
8	8	8	8	8	8	8	8	8
8	8	8	8	8	8	8	8	8
8	T	8	8	I	8	Z	8	8
8	8	E	8	8	8	8	8	D
W	8	8	H	8	8	E	8	8
8	8	N	8	8	8	I	8	8
A	8	8	M	8	8	E	8	I
8	G	8	8	H	8	T	8	8
8	8	8	8	8	8	8	8	8

SECRET CODE

Using the key below, decode the words that talk about baptism. *Solution on page 145.*

A = 🖊	H = 🏀	O = 🎓	V = 📘
B = ᴀBᴄ	I = ✒	P = 📜	W = ⚗
C = 📚	J = 🎒	Q = 🔬	X = 🎨
D = 🍎	K = 📕	R = 📕	Y = ✏
E = 🚌	L = 📎	S = 🖼	Z = 🏛
F = 📐	M = 🌍	T = 🖩	
G = 📝	N = 📖	U = 🎵	

1. __ __ __ __ __ __ __ __

2. __ __ __ __ __

3. __ __ __ __ __ __ __ __ __

4. __ __ __ __   __ __ __ __ __

5. __ __ __ __ __

6. __ __ __ __ __ __

WEEK 3

The Holy Ghost comforts and guides me.

Resources

Children's Songbook
The Still Small Voice (106)
Listen, Listen (107)

Hymns
The Spirit of God (2)
I Know My Father Lives (302)

Gospel Art Book
The Gift of the Holy Ghost (105)
Young Boy Praying (111)

Scriptures
Galatians 5:22–23
D&C 11:12

Lesson

Nephi and his brothers faced many challenges when they tried to obtain the brass plates from Laban. First, Laban stole the valuable items the brothers offered Laban for the plates. Then Laban tried to kill them. Laman and Lemuel were very angry, but Nephi knew they could not give up. Nephi went to Laban's house again, having faith that he would be guided and protected. He said, "And I was led by the Spirit, not knowing beforehand the things which I should do." Nephi was in a very scary situation, but he knew the Holy Ghost would be there to comfort him and guide him.

If we are worthy, the Holy Ghost will comfort and guide us. When we need help, He will guide us in making the right decision. When we are sad, He will help us feel the love of Heavenly Father and Jesus Christ. People feel the Holy Ghost in different ways. Some people hear a still, small voice. Others have thoughts come into their minds or feel strongly that they should do something. No matter how we feel the Holy Ghost, we will always feel good when the Holy Ghost is near.

Read (or summarize) and discuss 1 Nephi 4:6–38.
How did the Holy Ghost help Nephi?
How has the Holy Ghost guided and protected you?

Activity

All Ages: Play sounds your children are familiar with that signify an event: the phone ringing, the doorbell, the car starting, a timer, and so forth. Explain that these signs all represent something. For example, when the phone rings, we know someone wants to talk to us. Liken this to the promptings of the Holy Ghost. When we feel peace, the Holy Ghost is telling us to go ahead and do something. When we have a stupor of thought or a bad feeling, the Holy Ghost is warning us not to do something.

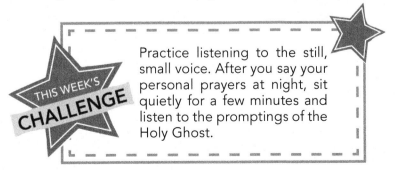

THIS WEEK'S CHALLENGE

Practice listening to the still, small voice. After you say your personal prayers at night, sit quietly for a few minutes and listen to the promptings of the Holy Ghost.

WEEK 4

I can know the truth through the power of the Holy Ghost.

Resources

Children's Songbook
The Holy Ghost (105)
Search, Ponder, and Pray (109)

Hymns
Testimony (137)
I Know My Father Lives (302)

Scriptures
John 15:26
3 Nephi 11:36

Lesson

It can be difficult to know if what we are taught is true. But God does not want us to remain confused. He has promised to send the Holy Ghost to help us.

When Lehi took his family into the wilderness, Nephi and his brothers wondered if their father really did have a vision that Jerusalem would be destroyed. Even though Nephi was righteous, leaving his home was difficult. But he prayed to know if his father's words were true, and the Holy Ghost comforted him and told him that they were (see 1 Nephi 2:16–17).

We can do the same. Whenever we have doubts about something being true (the scriptures, the words of the prophets, and so forth), we can pray and ask God. He will send the Holy Ghost to tell us what is right.

Read and discuss Moroni 10:3–5.

When we want to know the truth, do we simply ask God, or do we need to do something else first?

How does the Holy Ghost manifest the truth?

Activity

All Ages: Before family home evening begins, write a message to your children with invisible ink: Dip a Q-tip or paintbrush in some milk and write a message on a piece of paper. During family home evening, give your children the message written in invisible ink. Turn the stove on low, and help them hold it about twelve inches above the burner, until the message appears. (If the message does not appear, you may need to turn up the heat; however, be careful not to light the paper on fire.) Explain to your children that the heat from the stove is like the Holy Ghost. He helps us see things that are not obvious and tells us the truth of all things.

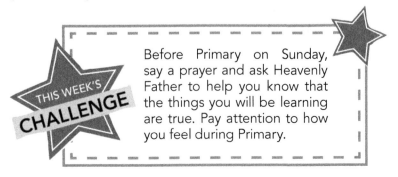

THIS WEEK'S CHALLENGE

Before Primary on Sunday, say a prayer and ask Heavenly Father to help you know that the things you will be learning are true. Pay attention to how you feel during Primary.

AUGUST

Participating in
Wholesome Activities
Will Strengthen
My Family

WEEK 1

"Pray in your families unto the Father" (3 Nephi 18:21).

Resources

Children's Songbook
A Child's Prayer (12)
I Pray in Faith (14)

Hymn
Did You Think to Pray? (140)

Gospel Art Book
In Favour with God (33)
Family Prayer (112)

Scriptures
1 John 3:22
Alma 37:37

Lesson

Jesus Christ taught the Nephites, "Pray in your families unto the Father, always in my name, that your wives and your children may be blessed" (3 Nephi 18:21). What do you think He meant? What types of blessings can we pray for?

The Church leaders have counseled us to pray as a family each morning and each night. When we do this, our love for each other grows and our bonds are strengthened. When we pray together for the same things, we become more unified and can feel the Spirit together.

We have also been counseled to pray individually, and husbands and wives should pray as a couple. This gives us an opportunity to pray for other family members and to seek personal guidance.

Jesus also taught us to "pray always, lest ye be tempted by the devil, and ye be led away captive by him" (3 Nephi 18:15). Prayer brings us a spiritual power that we can't get anywhere else.

Read and discuss Alma 34:19–27.
Where and when should we pray?
What are some of the things we can pray for?

Activity

Younger Children: The family on page 88 is saying a prayer. Draw a picture inside of the thought bubble of something you think they are praying for. You can download and print the activity at primaryhelper.com/downloads.

Older Children: See page 89. You can download and print the activity at primaryhelper.com/downloads.

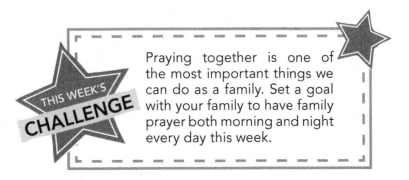

THIS WEEK'S CHALLENGE

Praying together is one of the most important things we can do as a family. Set a goal with your family to have family prayer both morning and night every day this week.

See how many words you can make from the phrase

PRAY IN YOUR
FAMILIES

_____   _____

_____   _____

_____   _____

_____   _____

_____   _____

_____   _____

_____   _____

_____   _____

WEEK 2

Family home evening strengthens my family.

Resources

Children's Songbook
The Family (194)
Family Night (195)

Hymns
Home Can Be a Heaven on Earth (298)
Families Can Be Together Forever (300)

Gospel Art Book
Family Prayer (112)

Scriptures
Deuteronomy 6:7
Moses 5:12

Lesson

Do you look forward to having family home evening each week? It's fun spending time together as a family, but there's more to it than fun activities and treats. The prophets have counseled us to have family home evening to strengthen our family. When we spend time together learning about the gospel, our testimonies grow together and we become more united.

Just over a hundred years ago, the prophet said we should set aside one night a week to hold family home evening. In 1970, President Joseph Fielding Smith said that we should hold family home evening on Monday nights, if possible.

Family home evening is a great time to set goals as a family and work together to achieve those goals. In addition, setting aside one night each week just for our family shows that it always comes first.

Read and discuss John 13:34.
How can we show love to our family members?
How does having family home evening strengthen our love for each other?

Activity

All Ages: Play Waddle Ball. Find a ball or a balloon and have two family members stand next to each other. Place the ball between the two people at their hips and have them walk across the room without dropping the ball or balloon. If they drop the ball, they must pick it up and start over. Take turns with the remaining family members to see who can carry the ball or balloon the farthest. After the game is over, discuss the importance of teamwork and working together as a family.

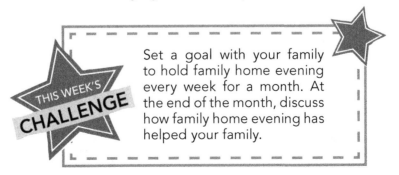

THIS WEEK'S CHALLENGE

Set a goal with your family to hold family home evening every week for a month. At the end of the month, discuss how family home evening has helped your family.

WEEK 3

Scripture study gives me and my family spiritual strength.

Resources

Children's Songbook
Search, Ponder, and Pray (109)
The Books in the Old Testament (114)

Hymns
As I Search the Holy Scriptures (277)
The Holy Word (279)

Gospel Art Book
Joseph Smith Seeks Wisdom
  from the Bible (89)

Scriptures
Isaiah 34:16
D&C 11:22

Lesson

How do you feel after eating a good breakfast? Do you feel strong and ready to tackle the day? Heavenly Father has given us food to fuel our physical bodies, and He has given us another type of food to fuel our spirits: the scriptures.

Studying the scriptures each day gives us the spiritual strength that we need to choose the right. But the word *study* is an important word. If we just read the scriptures quickly, without giving them much thought, we won't receive the strength that we need. It would be like eating only a couple bites of cereal and then running out the door and expecting to have enough energy to last all morning.

In the Book of Mormon, the prophet Nephi said that we should "feast upon the words of Christ" (2 Nephi 32:3). Let's read about that in 2 Nephi.

Read and discuss 2 Nephi 32:3.
What does it mean to "feast upon the words of Christ"?
What will the words of Christ tell us?

Activity

Younger Children: Draw a picture of your favorite scripture story.
Older Children: Have a scripture chase using scriptures that relate to the family. Look in the Topical Guide for ideas.

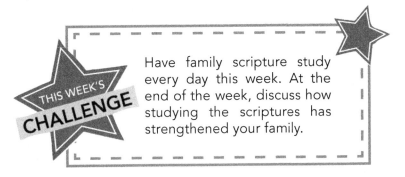

THIS WEEK'S CHALLENGE

Have family scripture study every day this week. At the end of the week, discuss how studying the scriptures has strengthened your family.

WEEK 4

The Sabbath is a day of rest and worship.

Resources

Children's Songbook
Remember the Sabbath Day (155)
Saturday (196)

Hymns
On This Day of Joy and Gladness (64)
Sabbath Day (148)

Gospel Art Book
Passing the Sacrament (108)

Scriptures
Exodus 20:8
Luke 23:56

Lesson

Heavenly Father has set apart the Sabbath day (Sunday) as a day of rest and a time when we can focus on worshiping. The most important thing we can do on the Sabbath day is attend all our church meetings and partake of the sacrament. But after we come home from church, we should still focus our thoughts on Heavenly Father.

Many of the activities we do during the week are not appropriate to do on Sunday. For example, if possible, parents should not go to work. We shouldn't shop or go to movies or sporting events.

Instead, we should do things that help us grow in the gospel or grow together as a family. We can read the scriptures or Church magazines, visit the sick, write in our journals, call family members, or do family history.

We may feel like we have to give up a lot on Sunday, but Heavenly Father will bless us if we keep the Sabbath day holy. Let's read about some of those blessings.

Read and discuss D&C 59:9–19.
How can we keep the Sabbath day holy?
What blessings will we receive for honoring the Sabbath day?

Activity

All Ages: Sometimes it can be hard to find things to do on Sunday afternoon. As a family, put together a Sabbath Day Kit. Find a box or a backpack and fill it with activities that are appropriate for the Sabbath day: a journal and a pen, stationery to write letters, appropriate books, appropriate music, and so on. You can make one kit for the entire family or one kit for each child.

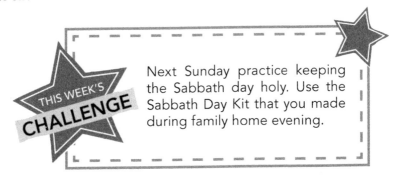

THIS WEEK'S CHALLENGE

Next Sunday practice keeping the Sabbath day holy. Use the Sabbath Day Kit that you made during family home evening.

SEPTEMBER

Living the Gospel
Blesses My Family

WEEK 1

I show my gratitude by showing thanks for all my blessings.

Resources

Children's Songbook
Thank Thee for Everything (10)
Thank Thee, Father (24)

Hymns
All Creatures of Our God and King (62)
I Stand All Amazed (193)

Scriptures
D&C 78:19
Alma 34:38

Lesson

How do you feel when you give someone a present or do something nice for them and they don't say thank you? That's how Heavenly Father feels when we don't thank Him. In the Doctrine and Covenants, we learn that ingratitude (not showing thanks) is one of the greatest sins (see D&C 59:21).

But there is more to gratitude than just saying, "thank you." Imagine that your parents bought you a brand new bike for your birthday. You were excited when you received it and told them thank you, but then you never rode it and acted like you didn't care about it. Your parents would feel sad and disappointed that you didn't like their gift.

Heavenly Father is sad when we don't read the scriptures or attend church. He has blessed us with many ways to draw closer to Him, and we need to show Him how grateful we are to have Him in our life.

Read and discuss D&C 59:21.

Why do you think ingratitude is such a great sin? How can we show our gratitude to Heavenly Father?

Activity

Younger Children: Write a thank you note to someone who has blessed your life. You can use the template on page 100 or create your own. You can download and print the activity at primaryhelper.com/downloads.

Older Children: Make a gratitude poster. Write a list or draw pictures of things that you are grateful for. Hang it somewhere your family will see it often, and continue to add to it throughout the week. You can use the template on page 101 or create your own. You can download and print the activity at primaryhelper.com/downloads.

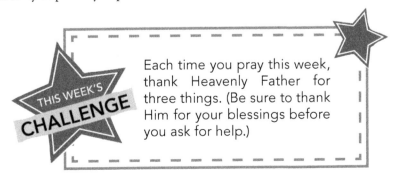

THIS WEEK'S CHALLENGE

Each time you pray this week, thank Heavenly Father for three things. (Be sure to thank Him for your blessings before you ask for help.)

WEEK 2

By giving service to others, I give service to God.

Resources

Children's Songbook
When We're Helping (198)
"Give," Said the Little Stream (236)

Hymns
Because I Have Been Given Much (219)
You Can Make the Pathway Bright (228)

Gospel Art Book
Service (115)

Scriptures
Mosiah 2:17
D&C 42:29

Lesson

Jesus spent His life serving others. He was the perfect example of how we can put others first. One day when He was tired, a group of people approached Him and wanted Him to bless their children. His Apostles wanted to send the people away and let Jesus rest, but He said, "Suffer little children, and forbid them not, to come unto me: for of such is the kingdom of heaven" (Matthew 19:14).

On another occasion, Jesus found out that John the Baptist had been killed. John was His cousin, so naturally Jesus was very sad. He went to the desert to be alone, but people followed Him (see Matthew 14:13–14). Jesus had compassion on them and healed them. Then He performed one of His great miracles and fed the five thousand with five loaves of bread and two fish.

Even though Jesus was tired and sad at times, He always put others first. He taught by word and example that those who will be saved at the last day are those who serve others. Let's read His words in Matthew 25.

Read and discuss Matthew 25:34–40.
What did Jesus mean when He said, "Inasmuch as ye have done it unto one of the least of these my brethren, ye have done it unto me"?
How can we serve our family members?
How are we serving God when we serve each other?

Activity

All Ages: Do a service project as a family. You could pick up trash at a park or school, help a neighbor with yard work, or take a meal to someone in need, and so on.

THIS WEEK'S CHALLENGE

Do a secret act of service for someone in your family or for a friend or neighbor.

WEEK 3

We believe in being honest.

Resources

Children's Songbook
The Thirteenth Article of Faith (132)
I Believe in Being Honest (149)

Hymns
Oh Say, What Is Truth? (272)
Truth Reflects upon Our Senses (273)

Scriptures
2 Nephi 9:34
D&C 51:9

Lesson

The first sentence of the thirteenth article of faith states, "We believe in being honest." What does it mean to be honest? Most people think of honesty as telling the truth. Not lying is a big part of honesty, but there's more to it than that. We need to be truthful in our actions as well as in our words.

You probably know that it is wrong to cheat in school or to steal. Did you know that cheating and stealing are forms of dishonesty? Other forms of dishonesty include pretending to be someone we are not or leading someone to believe something that is only half true.

At times it can be difficult to be honest. Sometimes being honest will get us in trouble. But no matter how much trouble we may get in, we should always tell the truth. Heavenly Father will be proud of us for being honest, and He will bless us for our efforts.

Read and discuss Articles of Faith 1:13.
What does it mean to be honest?
How do you feel when people are not honest with you?

Activity

Younger Children: Color the picture on page 106. You can download and print the activity at primaryhelper.com/downloads.

Older Children: See page 107. You can download and print the activity at primaryhelper.com/downloads.

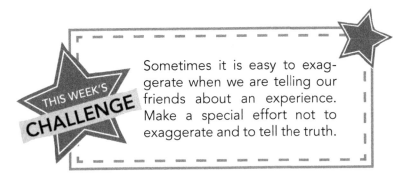

THIS WEEK'S CHALLENGE

Sometimes it is easy to exaggerate when we are telling our friends about an experience. Make a special effort not to exaggerate and to tell the truth.

I Show Honesty by Playing Fairly and Not Cheating

WHAT SHOULD I DO?

Pretend that you are the boy below and accidentally broke your mom's favorite vase. Write a story about what happened. How did the vase break? What do you tell your mom when she asks what happened? Do you choose to be honest or blame it on someone else?

_____

_____

_____

_____

_____

_____

_____

_____

_____

_____

_____

_____

_____

_____

_____

_____

WEEK 4

By living the gospel I set a good example for others to follow.

Resources

Children's Songbook
Jesus Wants Me for a Sunbeam (60)
Dare to Do Right (158)

Hymns
Each Life That Touches Ours for
Good (293)
Teach Me to Walk in the Light (304)

Scriptures
John 13:15
3 Nephi 15:12

Lesson

When Jesus gave the Sermon on the Mount, He said, "Let your light so shine before men, that they may see your good works, and glorify your Father which is in heaven" (Matthew 5:16). The light that Jesus was referring to is your testimony and example. He doesn't want you to hide your testimony of Him. He wants you to show the world what Christlike love is through your actions. When you live the gospel and help others (do "good works," as Jesus said), you set a good example for others to follow. Without using words, you teach others how to be kind, honest, and obedient.

People often don't comment on how we act, but they do notice how we behave. It is important that we always try our best to represent Jesus Christ. We never know how we may touch someone's life with our good example.

Read and discuss 1 Timothy 4:12.
Can you be a good example even if you are very young?
In what ways can you be a good example?

Activity

Younger Children: See page 110. In the sun, draw a picture of something you can do to be a good example. You can download and print the activity at primaryhelper.com/downloads.
Older Children: See page 111. You can download and print the activity at primaryhelper.com/downloads.

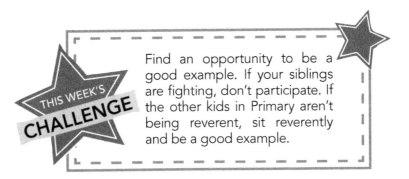

THIS WEEK'S CHALLENGE

Find an opportunity to be a good example. If your siblings are fighting, don't participate. If the other kids in Primary aren't being reverent, sit reverently and be a good example.

MISSING VOWELS

Below is a verse from the New Testament. Fill in the missing vowels to read a message from Jesus. *Solution on page 145.*

AAAAAA

EEEEEEEEEE   IIIIII

OOOOOOOOO   UUU

L _T   Y _ _R   L _GHT   S _

SH _N _   B _F _R _   M _N,

TH _T   TH _Y   M _Y   S _ _

Y _ _R   G _ _D   W _RKS,   _ND

GL _R _FY   Y _ _R   F _TH _R

WH _CH   _S   _N   H _ _V _N.

(M _TTH _W   5:16)

OCTOBER

"The Family: A Proclamation to the World" Came from God to Help My Family

WEEK 1

"The Family: A Proclamation to the World" came from God.

Resources

Children's Songbook
Love Is Spoken Here (190)
Because God Loves Me (234)

Hymns
O My Father (292)
Love at Home (294)

Gospel Art Book
Young Couple Going to the
Temple (120)

Scripture
"The Family: A Proclamation
to the World"

Lesson

Many people in the world do not value families the same way we do. Not everyone believes marriage is important or that a family should consist of a father and mother and their children. However, the prophets teach us differently. In 1995, the First Presidency and Quorum of the Twelve Apostles wrote a proclamation (letter) to the world. In it they talked about how important families are to God's plan.

President Hinckley read the proclamation during the General Relief Society meeting in Salt Lake City. He stated that "marriage between a man and a woman is ordained of God and that the family is central to the Creator's plan for the eternal destiny of His children" (first paragraph). The proclamation also mentions that each family member has sacred responsibilities.

Let's read the proclamation and discuss what we learn from it.

Read and discuss "The Family: A Proclamation to the World."
Why are families central to God's plan?
Why do you think the prophet and apostles gave this proclamation to the world?

Activity

All Ages: Watch the video of President Hinckley presenting the "Proclamation" to the members of the Church. It is available at www.lds.org/general-conference/1995/10/the-family-a-proclamation-to-the-world?lang=eng.

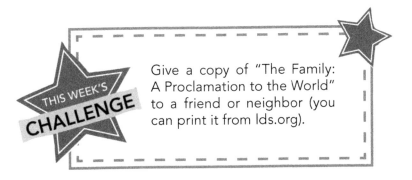

THIS WEEK'S CHALLENGE

Give a copy of "The Family: A Proclamation to the World" to a friend or neighbor (you can print it from lds.org).

WEEK 2

Marriage between a man and a woman is essential to God's plan.

Resources

Children's Songbook
I Love to See the Temple (95)
Where Love Is (138)

Hymns
Families Can Be Together Forever (300)
Love One Another (308)

Gospel Art Book
Young Couple Going to the Temple (120)
Salt Lake Temple (119)

Scriptures
"The Family: A Proclamation
   to the World"

Lesson

The first paragraph of "The Family: A Proclamation to the World" states, "We, the First Presidency and the Council of the Twelve Apostles of The Church of Jesus Christ of Latter-day Saints, solemnly proclaim that marriage between a man and a woman is ordained of God and that the family is central to the Creator's plan for the eternal destiny of His children."

Marriage between a man and a woman is essential to God's plan. When Adam and Eve were in the Garden of Eden, God married them as husband and wife. Adam and Eve were the first example of a loving husband and wife who obeyed the Lord's commandments.

The prophets have taught that marriages can be eternal (last forever) if they are performed by the proper authority. When a man and a woman are sealed in the temple, they will remain married to each other even after they die. Their children will also be theirs for eternity. The doctrine of eternal marriage is one of the most beautiful parts of the gospel. After the Atonement of Jesus Christ, our families are our most precious gift from Heavenly Father.

Read and discuss 1 Corinthians 11:11.
Why is marriage between a man and a woman essential to God's plan?
How can a marriage be eternal?

Activity

All Ages, Option 1: Look at wedding photos of your parents or grandparents. Talk about the importance of marriage.

All Ages, Option 2: Look at pictures of different temples at lds.org. Discuss why a temple marriage is essential to Heavenly Father's plan.

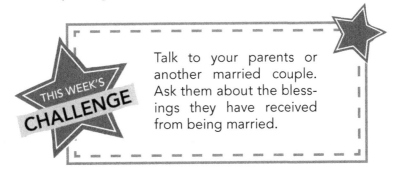

THIS WEEK'S CHALLENGE

Talk to your parents or another married couple. Ask them about the blessings they have received from being married.

WEEK 3

When family life is founded
on Jesus's teachings,
we can be happy.

Resources

Children's Songbook
Because God Loves Me (234)
Here We Are Together (261)

Hymns
How Firm a Foundation (85)
From Homes of Saints Glad Songs
    Arise (297)

Gospel Art Book
Jesus Knocking at the Door (65)
The Second Coming (66)

Scriptures
Helaman 5:12, D&C 6:34

Lesson

When Nephi and his family were searching for the promised land, the Lord told them, "Inasmuch as ye shall keep my commandments ye shall prosper in the land; but inasmuch as ye will not keep my commandments ye shall be cut off from my presence" (2 Nephi 1:20). The same promise applies to each of us. When we obey the commandments, Heavenly Father will bless us.

Following the teachings of Jesus Christ brings great joy. It is impossible to choose the right and feel bad. Sometimes choosing the right is hard—and we may have to give up something we want very much—but Heavenly Father will bless us for choosing the right. We may not see the blessings immediately, but they will always come.

Read and discuss Doctrine and Covenants 82:10.
Why is the Lord bound when we do what He says?
What does it mean to "have no promise"?
What are some of the blessings our family has received for following the teachings of Jesus Christ?

Activity

All Ages: Give each child two pieces of paper. Have them draw a happy face on one and a sad face on the other. Then read the statements on page 122 to your children. Have them decide if the family is following the teachings of Jesus Christ. If so, your children should hold up the happy face. If not, they should hold up the sad face.

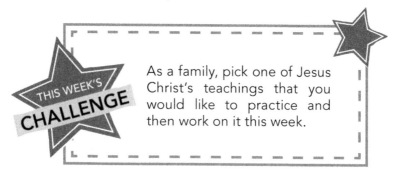

THIS WEEK'S CHALLENGE

As a family, pick one of Jesus Christ's teachings that you would like to practice and then work on it this week.

WEEK 4

Successful families work together.

Resources

Children's Songbook
A Happy Helper (197)
When We're Helping (198)

Hymns
Have I Done Any Good? (223)
The Time Is Far Spent (266)

Scriptures
Genesis 3:19
John 5:17

Lesson

Heavenly Father has taught us that working is important. He wants us to be responsible and provide for ourselves and our families. In the Doctrine and Covenants the Lord said, "Thou shalt not be idle; for he that is idle shall not eat the bread nor wear the garments of the laborer" (D&C 42:42). This scripture means that if we do not work, we should not expect to receive the rewards others have from working.

Successful families work together. It takes a lot to run a household. Parents are responsible for providing food, shelter, and clothing for their families. Children should help with chores that are appropriate for their age. Work doesn't have to be boring. If we have a good attitude and understand its purpose, we can enjoy it. And, most important, working together as a family builds strong relationships.

Read and discuss 2 Nephi 5:17.
What does it mean to be industrious?
How can we work together as a family?

Activity

All Ages: Do a chore or a project together. Make it fun by telling stories or singing songs while you work. Afterward have a treat or play a game as a reward.

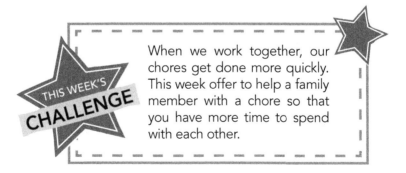

THIS WEEK'S CHALLENGE

When we work together, our chores get done more quickly. This week offer to help a family member with a chore so that you have more time to spend with each other.

When family life is founded on the teachings of Jesus Christ, we can be happy.

See page 119 for directions.

1. This family attends church every Sunday.
2. This family usually goes to church, but sometimes they miss it to attend sporting events.
3. This family likes to go out to eat after church on Sunday.
4. This family gets up early to read the scriptures together before work and school.
5. This family prays together daily.
6. This family has decided that they don't have enough money to pay tithing.
7. This family helps their elderly neighbor with his yard work once a week.
8. This family fasts if they aren't hungry when they wake up on fast Sunday.

NOVEMBER

Living the Teachings
of Jesus Christ
Strengthens Me
and My Family

WEEK 1

If ye have faith ye have hope.

Resources

Children's Songbook
I Pray in Faith (14)
Faith (96)

Hymns
Testimony (137)
I Know My Father Lives (302)

Scriptures
2 Corinthians 5:7
D&C 63:10

Lesson

In the Book of Mormon the prophet Alma taught, "If ye have faith ye hope for things which are not seen, which are true" (Alma 32:21). We cannot see Heavenly Father and Jesus Christ, but we can have faith that they are real. We cannot see the prophets from the scriptures, but we can have faith that they were good men and taught the word of God. We do not know what will happen in the future, but we can have faith that God will bless us with what we need.

Faith in Jesus Christ is the first principle of the gospel. Without faith, we cannot repent or become members of the Church. Without faith, we cannot find purpose in going to church or obeying the commandments. Sometimes it is difficult to believe in things we can't see, but each time we use our faith it will grow. In the Book of Mormon, the prophet Alma compared faith to a seed. A seed may be small, but if you nourish it and care for it properly, it can grow into something big and beautiful.

Read and discuss Alma 32:28.
How is faith like a seed?
How can we make our faith grow?

Activity

All Ages: Plant a seed in a small pot or a paper cup. Water it according to the package instructions and check on its progress daily. Discuss with your family how taking care of this seed is like nourishing your faith.

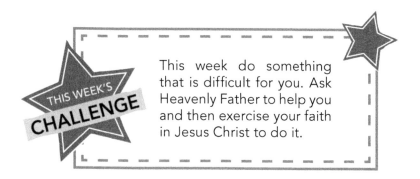

THIS WEEK'S CHALLENGE

This week do something that is difficult for you. Ask Heavenly Father to help you and then exercise your faith in Jesus Christ to do it.

WEEK 2

Prayer is reverent communication with Heavenly Father.

Resources

Children's Songbook
Love Is Spoken Here (190)
Family Prayer (189)

Hymns
Did You Think to Pray? (140)
Secret Prayer (144)

Scriptures
Matthew 6:6
Thessalonians 5:17

Lesson

Has your father ever gone a trip without you? How did you feel? Did he seem far away because you couldn't see him? If you were able to talk to him on the phone, you were probably excited to tell him about what was happening in your life. Do you ever feel that Heavenly Father is far away because you can't see Him? It may seem that way at times, but Heavenly Father is only as far away as we make Him. We can always talk to Heavenly Father through prayer, and the Holy Ghost will tell us that He's listening.

Heavenly Father wants us to pray to Him each day. He wants to know what is going on in our lives, and He wants us to ask Him for help. We can pray to Heavenly Father to know if the scriptures are true, or we can ask Him to help us find something that we lost. We should also pray and give thanks to Heavenly Father. Everything that we have comes from Him, and we need to show that we are grateful. Even though we may not hear Heavenly Father's voice speaking to us when we pray, we can feel the Holy Ghost. This is Heavenly Father's way of letting us know that He hears our prayers.

Read and discuss Doctrine and Covenants 19:28.
What does it mean to pray in your heart?
How does Heavenly Father hear us, even when we don't pray out loud?

Activity

All Ages: Make a telephone with soup cans and string (see page 132 for instructions). Go in different rooms and take turns talking to each other. Explain to your children that even though we can't see Heavenly Father, we can pray to Him anytime, anywhere. He will always hear and answer our prayers.

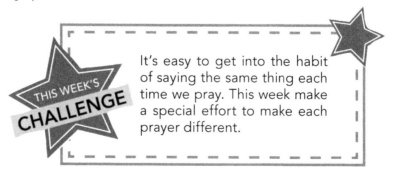

THIS WEEK'S CHALLENGE

It's easy to get into the habit of saying the same thing each time we pray. This week make a special effort to make each prayer different.

WEEK 3

Repentance is a change of mind and heart.

Resources

Children's Songbook
Repentance (98)
The Fourth Article of Faith (124)

Hymns
Come unto Jesus (117)
As Now We Take the Sacrament (169)

Scriptures
2 Nephi 2:21
D&C 58:42

Lesson

The only way to return to Heavenly Father is to follow Jesus Christ and keep all the commandments. But when He sent us to earth, Heavenly Father knew we would not always choose the right. He provided a Savior for us so we can repent of our sins and be forgiven. Because Jesus Christ died for us, we can be washed clean from our sins.

We must take certain steps to be forgiven. First, we admit that we made a mistake and feel godly sorrow for our sins. There is a difference between feeling godly sorrow and feeling sorrow because we have to face the consequences of our sins.

Second, we forsake, or stop, our sins. If we have lied, we must stop lying.

Third, we confess our sins to Heavenly Father and anyone else that we have hurt. If we called someone a bad name, we must confess that sin to both Heavenly Father and the person we hurt.

Fourth, we make restitution. We correct the wrong act. If we have stolen something, we return the item to the owner or find a way to pay for it.

Fifth, we forgive others. God can't forgive us if we don't forgive others.

Finally, we keep the commandments of God. We are not fully repentant if we don't continue doing our best to choose the right. We must have a change of heart and lose our desire to sin.

Repentance can be hard, but we will find great joy in giving up our sins and following Jesus Christ.

Read and discuss Isaiah 1:18.
What are scarlet and crimson?
How does the turning of these colors to white represent repentance?

Activity

All Children: Put a lemon in a bowl of water and explain to your children that lemons float in water. Push the lemon down to show that it will pop back up and float. Cut the lemon in small pieces. The pieces will still float. Then remove the skin from each piece of lemon. The pieces will now sink. Liken the lemon to ourselves and repentance. The skin of the lemon is like our sins. As long as we are holding on to our sins, we cannot truly repent and be cleansed. But when we shed our sins, we can "sink" into the water, just like the pieces of lemon did, and be cleansed from our sins.

WEEK 4

Forgiveness brings peace.

Resources

Children's Songbook
Help Me, Dear Father (99)
I'm Trying to Be like Jesus (78)

Hymns
Prayer Is the Soul's Sincere Desire (145)
Father in Heaven, We Do Believe (180)

Gospel Art Book
The Crucifixion (57)
The Lost Lamb (64)

Scriptures
1 Nephi 7:21
Luke 23:34

Lesson

In the Book of Mormon we read about a man named Enos and his experience with repentance. One day Enos was hunting in the forest and started thinking about the gospel truths that his father, Jacob, had taught him. Enos felt a great desire in his heart to repent of his sins. He knelt down in the forest and began to pray. Let's read about his experience.

Read and discuss Enos 1:4–8.
How did Enos know his sins were forgiven?
Why was his guilt swept away?

Activity

All Ages: Have a child wear an empty backpack. The other children take turns putting a rock, a book, or another heavy object inside. As each item is placed in the backpack, the child names a sin (name-calling, disobeying parents, and so on). When the backpack is full, ask the child to walk across the room. He may not be able to do it, and if he can, it will be difficult. Explain how sins weigh us down and make it hard for us to "walk" back to Heavenly Father. Then, one by one, remove each "sin" from the backpack. Explain how repentance lightens our load and brings peace. You may want to read Matthew 11:28 and discuss how the Savior carries our burdens.

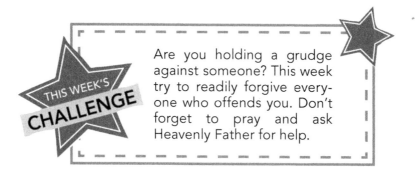

THIS WEEK'S CHALLENGE

Are you holding a grudge against someone? This week try to readily forgive everyone who offends you. Don't forget to pray and ask Heavenly Father for help.

CAN YOU HEAR ME?

Materials
2 identical soup cans
pointed tool*
5-foot length of string
toothpick (optional)

Instructions
1. In the bottom of each can, punch a small hole. The hole should be big enough for the string to go through but small enough that it won't fall out when knotted.
2. Insert the string through the hole in one of the cans. Tie a knot and pull the string tight. If the knot is not big enough and the string slips through the hole, tie the string around a toothpick to hold the string in place.
3. Repeat step 2 with the remaining can and the other end of the string.

* To avoid injury, parents should help children punch holes with the pointed tool.

DECEMBER

We Remember and
Worship Our Savior,
Jesus Christ

WEEK 1

The sacrament is a time to remember Jesus Christ.

Resources

Children's Songbook
To Think about Jesus (71)
Before I Take the Sacrament (73)

Hymns
As Now We Take the Sacrament (169)
While of These Emblems We Partake (173)

Gospel Art Book
Blessing the Sacrament (107)
Passing the Sacrament (108)

Scriptures
John 6:54
D&C 59:9

Lesson

When we are baptized, we promise to follow Jesus Christ. As much as we want to follow Him, we still sin afterward. Fortunately, we can always repent of our sins. We should repent often, even daily if necessary.

Each Sunday we renew our baptismal covenants when we take the sacrament. Although we are baptized only once, we can recommit (promise again) each week to choose the right.

You have probably noticed that the chapel is very quiet during the sacrament. That is because the sacrament is a sacred ordinance. We need to focus our thoughts on Jesus and think about how we can better follow Him. And we need to be quiet so that those around us can do the same.

During the sacrament, some people read from the hymnbook or from their scriptures. Others like to just think about what Jesus Christ means to them. Whatever you choose to do, make sure that your thoughts are focused on Jesus and His sacrifice for us. Think about what you can do that week to be a better disciple of Jesus Christ.

Read and discuss the sacrament prayers in Doctrine and Covenants 20:77, 79.
What covenants do we renew when we take the sacrament?
What does God promise us if we keep our covenants?

Activity

All Ages: Make Christmas cards to send to friends or relatives. Include your testimony of the Savior.

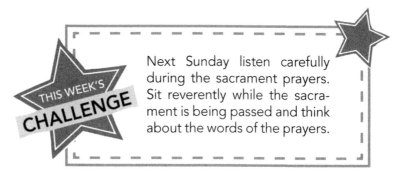

THIS WEEK'S CHALLENGE

Next Sunday listen carefully during the sacrament prayers. Sit reverently while the sacrament is being passed and think about the words of the prayers.

WEEK 2

Remembering Jesus Christ helps me choose the right.

Resources

Children's Songbook
Stand for the Right (159)
Choose the Right Way (160)

Hymns
Do What Is Right (237)
Choose the Right (239)

Gospel Art Book
Christ's Image (1)
Christ with Children (116)

Scriptures
Joshua 24:15
Psalm 119:30

Lesson

Each day we are faced with choices. We must decide if we will pray that day, read the scriptures, be obedient, be kind to others, and so on. Sometimes we may be tempted to do other things instead. When we remember Jesus Christ's example, it will be much easier to choose the right.

Jesus lived a perfect life and always chose the right, even when He was in difficult situations. When He fasted for forty days, He was extremely hungry. Satan tempted Him to turn stones into bread. But Jesus did not give in.

When Jesus was in the Garden of Gethsemane, He felt great pain. All the sins of the world were upon Him. He wanted to give up, but He wanted to obey Heavenly Father more. Let's read about His experience.

Read and discuss Luke 22:41–44.
Why did Jesus endure such great pain?
How can remembering Jesus help you choose the right?

Activity

All Ages: On page 144 you will find a template to make a small box like the one shown. Print the template on heavy paper, cut along the solid lines, and then fold on the dotted lines to make the box. Put a small treat or gift in the box and give it to someone who could use some Christmas cheer. You can download and print the template at primaryhelper.com/downloads.

THIS WEEK'S CHALLENGE

Memorize the song "Jesus Once Was a Little Child" (*Children's Songbook,* 55).

WEEK 3

The Son of God was born on earth.

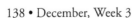

Lesson

Read and discuss the story of Christ's birth in Luke 2:1–19.
Why did the angel tell the shepherds not to fear?
Why was Jesus born in a manger?

Activity

Younger Children: See page 140. In the ornament, draw a picture of Jesus's birth. You can download and print the activity at primaryhelper .com/downloads.

Older Children: See page 141. You can download and print the activity at primaryhelper.com/downloads.

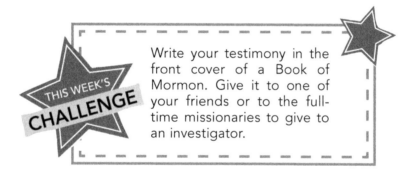

THIS WEEK'S CHALLENGE

Write your testimony in the front cover of a Book of Mormon. Give it to one of your friends or to the full-time missionaries to give to an investigator.

CHRISTMAS CODE

Each number on the Christmas tree represents a letter. Determine which letter each number represents, and then unscramble the letters to spell a word about Christmas. **Solution on page 145.**

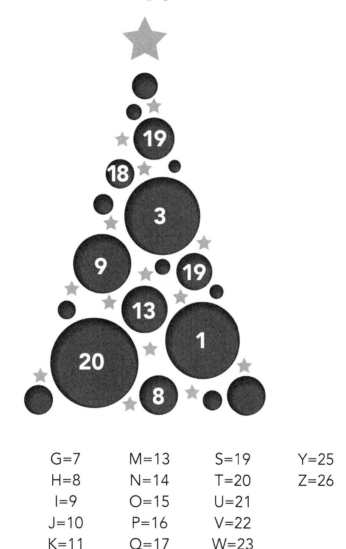

A=1	G=7	M=13	S=19	Y=25
B=2	H=8	N=14	T=20	Z=26
C=3	I=9	O=15	U=21	
D=4	J=10	P=16	V=22	
E=5	K=11	Q=17	W=23	
F=6	L=12	R=18	X=24	

___ ___ ___ ___ ___ ___ ___ ___ ___ ___

WEEK 4

Jesus will come again.

Resources

Children's Songbook
When He Comes Again (82)
The Tenth Article of Faith (128)

Hymns
The Spirit of God (2)
Now Let Us Rejoice (3)

Gospel Art Book
The Second Coming (66)

Scriptures
2 Thessalonians 1:7
D&C 1:12

Lesson

After Jesus was resurrected, He taught His disciples that even though He would soon return to His Father, He would come to earth again. But no one would know when that would be. Jesus said, "But of that day and hour knoweth no man, no, not the angels of heaven, but my Father only" (Matthew 24:36).

Latter-day prophets have taught that the Second Coming will take place soon. But we still do not know when that day will come. We need to live righteously and be ready to meet Jesus. It will be a glorious day for those who are prepared.

In the New Testament, Jesus gave a parable of the ten virgins. These women were waiting for the bridegroom to come. Five of them were prepared to see him, and five were not. Let's read about them.

Read and discuss Matthew 25:1–13.
Who do the ten virgins represent?
What can we do to prepare for the Second Coming?

Activity

All Ages: As a family, set some goals for the new year. Put the list on the refrigerator or somewhere your family will see it often.

THIS WEEK'S CHALLENGE

Watch the news or read the newspaper with your family and discuss some of the events that show the Second Coming is drawing near.

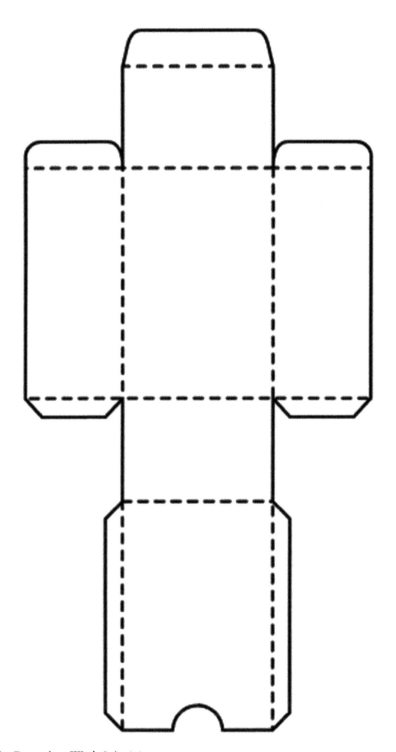

ANSWER KEY

PAGE 5

```
A S J Z O N R I G̶O̶D̶ L M
H I G̶L̶O̶R̶I̶F̶I̶E̶D̶ Q R
Z B C X W D A H B E I C F
C̶ G̶ S̶ P̶ I̶ R̶ I̶ T̶ D J H E I
H K J F T M K I G A H I L
R A M H N N J O P M K Q R
  S L O E B T J E M U L V
S C E Q S N D R K W O T X
T P Y N S Z D A R Q R B C
D F P E S L C F T G U F H
I V J A W X K X Z L Y M
N Z O H A P B Q S̶R̶I̶E̶H̶
R S C D G T D E U F V G W
```

PAGE 43

```
N A N B M B F D S C G O D
  E G̶R̶A̶N̶D̶M̶A̶ F R M E
E G̶M̶O̶M̶ G H A U E A I O
C P A T B B A K N H N O N
E A K H C I C F T U D B E
C R H E J H D R C K P L P
E F M R G L Q N B H A O H
C̶O̶U̶S̶I̶N̶ P R I D L J E
K S Q D U L I V E R A M W
F S N D̶A̶D̶ T G O T P U G
C Q E H R V U G W K S I X
Q T W Z B C S B U G R I L
E̶L̶C̶N̶U̶ M R T Q X C B S
```

PAGE 11

EXAMPLE

PAGE 67

PAGE 21

1. DAY, NIGHT
2. CLOUDS, OCEANS
3. LAND, PLANTS, TREES
4. SUN, MOON, STARS
5. FISH, BIRDS, ANIMALS
6. MAN

PAGE 79

COVENANT
EIGHT
IMMERSION
HOLY GHOST
CHURCH
JESUS
FAITH
REPENT

PAGE 25

PAGE 111

LET YOUR LIGHT SO SHINE
BEFORE MEN, THAT THEY
MAY SEE YOUR GOOD WORKS,
AND GLORIFY YOUR FATHER
WHICH IS IN HEAVEN.
(MATTHEW 5:16)

PAGE 141

CHRISTMAS

FUN TREATS
FOR FHE

Simple, Kid-Friendly Recipes

These recipes may not be fancy, but they're simple, fun treats that children of all ages will enjoy making and eating.

Cake Mix
Sandwich Cookies

INGREDIENTS

1 box cake mix of your choice
2 eggs
½ cup vegetable oil
1 small tub vanilla frosting

INSTRUCTIONS

1. Mix together all ingredients except frosting.
2. Roll dough into little balls. Place on ungreased cookie sheet.
3. Bake at 350 degrees for 8–10 minutes.
4. When cookies are completely cool, make sandwiches by frosting a cookie and placing another one on top.

Ice Cream Float

INGREDIENTS

vanilla ice cream
your favorite soda

INSTRUCTIONS

1. Scoop ice cream into a cup or malt glass.

2. Pour your favorite soda on top.

Strawberry Shortcake

INGREDIENTS

3–4 cups fresh strawberries, sliced
sugar to taste
1 angel food cake (or cake of your choice), sliced
1 carton whipped topping

INSTRUCTIONS

1. Mix together strawberries and sugar to desired sweetness.
2. Top slice of cake with strawberries and a dollop of whipped topping.

Waffle Sundae

INGREDIENTS

1 box cake mix of your choice
eggs, oil, and water (amount varies with each mix)
ice cream or whipped topping
your favorite sundae toppings

INSTRUCTIONS

1. Prepare cake mix according to package directions.
2. Bake individual portions of the mix in a waffle iron instead of in the oven.
3. Top each waffle with ice cream (or whipped topping) and your favorite sundae toppings.

Chocolate-Dipped Pretzels

INGREDIENTS

1 cup chocolate chips
2 tsp. Crisco
6 pretzel rods
½ cup chopped nuts (optional)
½ cup crushed candy (optional)

INSTRUCTIONS

1. Mix together chocolate chips and Crisco in a microwave-safe bowl. Microwave on high for about one minute or until chocolate is melted.

2. Remove bowl from microwave. Stir until smooth.

3. Place a sheet of wax paper on the counter or on a cookie sheet. Dip each pretzel into melted chocolate, leaving one end uncovered. Place dipped pretzels on wax paper. Sprinkle with chopped nuts or crushed candy, if desired.

4. Place pretzels in refrigerator for 15–20 minutes or until chocolate hardens.